Larry Gets Lost in Prehistoric Times

From Dinosaurs to the Stone Age

Illustrated by John Skewes
Written by Andrew Fox and John Skewes

SASQUATCH BOOKS
SEATTLE

Manufactured in China by C&C Offset Printing Co. Ltd. Shanghai, China, in May 2013

Published by Sasquatch Books
17 16 15 14 13   9 8 7 6 5 4 3 2 1

Editor: Susan Roxborough
Project editor: Michelle Hope Anderson
Illustrations: John Skewes
Book design: Mint Design
Book composition: Sarah Plein

Library of Congress Cataloging-in-Publication Data is available.

ISBN: 978-1-57061-862-8

Sasquatch Books
1904 Third Avenue, Suite 710
Seattle, WA 98101
(206) 467-4300
www.sasquatchbooks.com
custserv@sasquatchbooks.com

This is **Larry.**   And this is **Pete.**

Pete reads aloud while Larry rests at his feet.

This afternoon Pete has homework to do.
To read about history, then write a page or two.

Larry dozes off as Pete reads away.
Dreaming of wonderful places to play.

"Long, long ago
Before your grandparents' birth
Giant creatures called dinosaurs
Made homes here on Earth."

What's this? Larry wondered,
Blinking his eyes . . .

MESOZOIC Era

251 to 65.5 million years ago

A creature so big
It reached up to the sky!

Larry ran around
Its **enormous** feet.
Lucky for him, this guy
Doesn't eat meat.

BRACHIOSAURUS

A big plant-eating dinosaur called a sauropod, among the biggest creatures to ever walk the earth. They could be 85 feet from nose to tail and weigh more than 30 tons.

But soon he was running from
Some creatures that *DO!*

TYRANNOSAURUS REX
One of the biggest meat eaters to
ever live, they could be more than
40 feet from nose to tail and weigh
more than 8 tons. A single tooth
could be 12 inches long.

VELOCIRAPTORS
Small meat-eating dinosaurs that walked on two legs.
Paleontologists (scientists who study the fossils of dinosaurs
and other ancient life) think they were able to run very fast.

And Larry thinks **THIS** one
Is a meat eater, too!

He quickly takes off
In the **other** direction.
These big guys with horns
Might offer protection.

e name Tyrannosaurus
s "tyrant lizard", from the
k words tyrannos meaning
nt", and sauros meaning
d". The Tyrannosaurus rex
x meaning "king" in Latin);

TRICERATOPS
The name means "three-horned face." About 9 feet tall and 25 feet long, the Triceratops has one of the largest skulls of any land creature.

As Pete reads on,
He learns about different stages,
And how creatures appear
And change through the ages.

These guys look scary,
With armor and spikes.
But that's just for defense;
It's plants that they like.

EUOPLOCEPHALUS

CENTROSAURUS

REPTILES
Just like modern birds,
baby dinosaurs were
hatched from eggs.

PACHYCEPHALOSAURUS

But not all these creatures
Are so large in size,
Some are covered in feathers . . .

OVIRAPTOROSAUR

SINORNITHOSAURUS

And others can fly!

IBEROMESORNIS

This one's so small
He can rest on a twig . . .

QUETZALCOATLUS

One of the largest flying animals of all
time. Its wingspan could measure 36 feet.

While others, he found,
Are still very **big**.

ELASMOSAURUS
With a very long neck (more than 70 vertebrae!), they reached 46 feet in length and weighed more than 4,400 pounds.

MOSASAUR
A large carnivorous sea lizard with sharp teeth.

He squirmed and he wiggled, until he was free.
Then—**splash!**—he found himself under the sea!

Larry could scarcely believe his dog eyes:
There were more creatures here, of every possible size.

He swam toward land with all the strength in his paws.
Even faster when he saw sharp teeth and big jaws!

SHARKS, SEA TURTLES, AND COELACANTHS
These are examples of Cretaceous creatures
that still live today.

AMMONITE

Larry climbed from the water
And time seemed to change.
Many years had passed,
This was a new age.

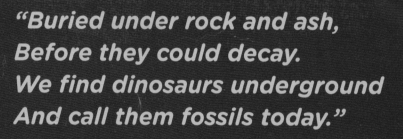

"Buried under rock and ash,
Before they could decay.
We find dinosaurs underground
And call them fossils today."

CRETACEOUS-PALEOGENE EXTINCTION EVENT
65.5 million years ago

CRETACEOUS

JURASSIC

TRIASSIC

FOSSILS
If something becomes buried under
the right conditions, the evidence of
it can last for millions of years.

CENOZOIC Era

65.5 million years ago to today

Much of the earth was covered
With snow and with ice.
More furry animals appeared,
Some huge, some small as mice.

MAMMALS
While some warm-blooded animals
with fur existed in the age of
dinosaurs, they became larger and
more plentiful in the Cenozoic era.

ICE AGE
There have been several ice ages.
The last one was 15,000 years
ago. Glaciers covered much of the
earth, covering oceans and carving
out mountains as they went.

WOOLLY MAMMOTH

Wait a minute!
This guy has no fur at all.
And compared with those other giants,
He looks rather small.

Eventually the ice
Began to recede,
Which made it much easier
For animals to feed.

MODERN HUMANS
Scientists estimate that Homo sapiens, the first modern humans, appeared about 200,000 years ago.

Prehistoric people had to
Get by on their own.
They learned how to make *FIRE*
And tools out of stone.

Life must have been hard,
And they had to be brave.
To hide from beasts,
Some made homes in caves.

STONE AGE

The age of stone tools and the discovery of fire mark the beginning of modern humans. Gradually, the first farms would be settled and some wolves would be the start of domesticated dogs!

But they could make artwork
On the walls of their caves.
These paintings can still
Be seen to this day.

As Larry goes deeper into the cave
The air seems to get thinner.

Wait, what's that?
Kind of smells like . . .

dinner!

All of a sudden
Larry awakes from his nook.

He wasn't lost in time,
It was only a book!

He goes to the window—
No dinosaurs around.
Look as he might
There's not one to be found.

It looks a lot like any other day.
The dinosaurs are gone . . .

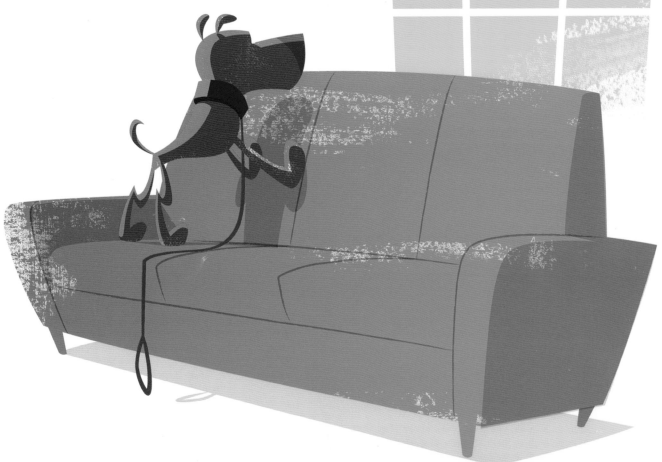

Or are they?